The Family's First Puppy

Maryann Mott

Contents

Photo Credits: Isabelle Francais

© T.F.H. Publications, Inc.

Distributed in the UNITED STATES to the Pet Trade by T.F.H. Publications, Inc., 1 TFH Plaza, Neptune City, NJ 07753; on the Internet at www.tfh.com; in CANADA by Rolf C. Hagen Inc., 3225 Sartelon St., Montreal, Quebec H4R 1E8; Pet Trade by H & L Pet Supplies Inc., 27 Kingston Crescent, Kitchener, Ontario N2B 2T6; in ENGLAND by T.F.H. Publications, PO Box 74, Havant PO9 5TT; in AUSTRALIA AND THE SOUTH PACIFIC by T.F.H. (Australia), Pty. Ltd., Box 149, Brookvale 2100 N.S.W., Australia; in NEW ZEALAND by Brooklands Aquarium Ltd., 5 McGiven Drive, New Plymouth, RD1 New Zealand; in SOUTH AFRICA by Rolf C. Hagen S.A. (PTY.) LTD., P.O. Box 201199, Durban North 4016, South Africa; in Japan by T.F.H. Publications. Published by T.F.H. Publications, Inc.

MANUFACTURED IN THE
UNITED STATES OF AMERICA
BY T.F.H. PUBLICATIONS, INC.

Things to Consider

t's easy to fall in love with a small, furry puppy. For some people, all it takes is just one look, but don't rush in to adopting. You need to think about this with your head and not your heart—and that can be tough with those big, brown puppy eyes looking up at you. In order to make the right decision, you'll need to honestly answer a few questions: Will you have time to spend with your new friend? Can you afford to care for him properly? Do you live in a place that allows pets?

If you decide to bring a puppy into your life, you'll need to know where to find a canine friend, how to train him, groom and care for him, and, if you have children, how to teach them to be responsible owners.

This book will help you to answer all these questions and more.

ARE YOU READY?

Getting a puppy is a lot like getting married. It means sticking it out through the good times and bad, in sickness and in health, till death do you part. Okay, maybe that's a bit much, but you get the picture. Most dogs live until they're approximately 12 years old. That adds up to a lot of walks around the neighborhood, not to mention a lot of dog food over the years. Consider the following questions carefully, because they will help you to decide whether or not to take the plunge.

1. Do you rent? If the answer is yes, get your landlord's permission before adopting or buying a dog. If you own a house or condominium governed by an association, find out the rules regarding pets. Some associations limit the number you can own, prohibit certain breeds, or don't allow dogs at all.

2. Do you have enough space? A big fenced-in backyard is ideal. At minimum, you'll need a safe area to walk your puppy. Allowing your dog to run loose is never an option. He could get hit by a car or get into a fight with another dog, both of which will cost you medical bills and heartache—not to mention the fact that you'll be extremely unpopular with your neighbors.

3. Can you afford it? The expenses don't stop after purchasing the puppy. In fact, it's just the beginning. The costs can include a monthly trip to the groomer, spay or neuter surgery, vaccinations, good-quality commercial dog food, flea control (three-month supply), and obedience classes. Then there are collars, leashes, bowls, toys,

An energetic puppy needs a lot of space to run and to exercise his growing limbs. A large, fenced-in yard is ideal and keeps him out of danger.

Puppies and children make great playmates. However, children cannot take on the sole responsibility of caring for a dog, so be sure that you want a pet as much as your child does.

THINGS TO CONSIDER

license fees, and the unexpected injuries or illnesses. Take all these expenses (plus the ones you can't think of ahead of time) into consideration.

4. Is this puppy for you or your child? Don't get a puppy just because your child wants one. Children are not capable of performing all the day-to-day pet care responsibilities, no matter how hard they try to convince you otherwise. The majority of care will fall into your hands, so if you have no interest in getting a dog—don't get one.

5. Do you move frequently? Finding a place to live that accepts pets can be difficult, so it's best to hold off adopting a puppy until you've settled down.

6. Do you work long hours? You'll need to spend at least two hours each day caring for your pet, which includes feeding, walking, and grooming. You'll also want to have enough time to play together. Spending a couple of hours after work with your new best friend will help you to unwind after a long day. The best part is when the weekend rolls around. There are tons of cool things you can do together—hiking, biking, walking, and jogging are just some of them.

7. Are you allergic? About 15 percent of the US population is allergic to animals. That figure doubles for those with asthma. How do you know if you are allergic? Symptoms usually occur about 15 minutes after being near a dog. Some people, however, have a delayed reaction several hours later. If there is a chance you or someone in your family might be allergic, consult your doctor about having an allergy test done.

Well, you've answered all the questions and feel that you're ready—for better or worse—to own a puppy. Great! Bringing a dog into your life is a lot of work, especially in the beginning, but the love, laughs, and friendship you'll share will make it all worthwhile.

Do not get a pet unless you have the time and energy to feed him, walk him, and groom him. He will also look to you for a fun playmate.

SELECTING THE PERFECT PUPPY

Should you buy a purebred from a breeder or adopt a mixed breed from the local shelter? It's really a matter of preference, because both can make great companions.

Purebred Puppies

There are more than 140 breeds of purebred dog ranging from the pint-sized Chihuahua to the gentle, gigantic Irish Wolfhound. Owning a purebred means that you can expect certain physical and behavioral qualities. This makes it easier when trying to choose the right puppy for your family because there won't be any surprises. You'll know exactly what to expect as far as how he'll look and act when fully grown.

The downside is that congenital problems are common. Breeds with pushed-in faces, like Pugs and Pekingese, are susceptible to respiratory problems and heatstroke. Some large- and medium-sized breeds like Chow Chows, German Shepherds, Bulldogs, and St. Bernards are prone to hip dysplasia. Akitas, Cocker Spaniels, and Siberian Huskies are predisposed to cataracts, and deafness often affects Dalmatians.

The way to avoid these problems is to buy a puppy from a reputable breeder that has a history of responsible breeding, belongs to the breed's club, and is aware of the problems that exist in the breed. Make sure the puppy and his parents have been tested for congenital diseases. For example, a puppy examined by a certified ophthalmologist and found to be free of major heritable eye diseases can be registered with the Canine Eye Registry Foundation (CERF). To check for deafness, a brain stem auditory evoked response test (BAER) can be performed, and to detect hip or elbow dysplasia, the Orthopedic Foundation for Animals (OFA) offers a diagnostic service.

If you want a purebred puppy but don't know what breed would be best for your family, take the puppy picker test at www.selectsmart.com. This interactive website asks several questions and gives you a list of suitable breeds based on your answers. Another great website is Ralston Purina's breed selector at www.purina.com/dogs/index.html. This also prompts you through a series of questions and puts together a list of breeds that are right for you. The neat thing about this site is that it shows pictures of each breed as well as offers information on size, activity level, trainability, temperament, and grooming requirements.

If you don't have Internet access, *The Complete Dog Book* by the American Kennel Club, *Choosing a Dog for Life*, published by T. F. H. Publications, or the *Encyclopedia of Dog Breeds* by D. Caroline Coile are good sources. All have pictures and descriptions to help narrow down your search for the perfect puppy.

Shelters

Custom-blended canines can also be a great choice. They're less expensive to buy and have fewer genetic problems. Best of all, when you adopt from a shelter, you're saving a life. You can also take pride in knowing your mixed breed is one-of-a-kind. There will never be another with his unique beauty. The downside is that there's no way to gauge how big he will grow or what his temperament will be like.

Other Considerations

Whether you select a purebred or a mixed breed, here are some other things to take into consideration during your search for the perfect pup.

Activity Level: To become best friends with your puppy, you'll need to spend time together. That means picking a dog with an energy level that is similar to yours. For example, if you're a couch potato, select a breed that doesn't require a lot of exercise, like a Chihuahua, Bichon Frise, or Bulldog. On the other hand, if you like to go jogging or hiking, an energetic Dalmatian, Golden Retriever, or Jack Russell Terrier might be your perfect pooch.

Male or Female: Both sexes will protect your house and provide plenty of love. If you don't spay or neuter your pet, gender does make a difference. Whole male dogs will roam neighborhoods and get into territorial fights with other males. When unspayed females come into heat, they secrete a bloody discharge and attract every male in the area. The best thing to do for your pet's health and well-being is to have him or her spayed or neutered.

Coat: It's hard to resist a fluffy, furry pup, but all that hair requires a lot of upkeep. Breeds like Cocker Spaniels, Old English Sheepdogs, or Shih Tzus need regular visits to the groomer.

If you're not willing to spend the money on grooming, choose a short-haired breed, like a Jack Russell Terrier, Rottweiler, or Beagle. These breeds still need to be brushed and bathed on a regular basis, but their coats don't have to be trimmed, so most owners can easily handle the grooming regimen at home.

Timing: Try to adopt during the warm summer months when the kids are out of school and have extra time to help the puppy adjust to his new home. Summer's pleasant temperatures also make housetraining easier. Let's face it, standing in the middle of a snowstorm waiting for your puppy to relieve himself is not fun. Also, try to arrange to bring your dog home at the start of a weekend or at the beginning of a vacation. This way you can spend as much time with your puppy as possible before returning to work or school.

There are so many great pets in need of loving homes. Adopting a mixed breed from a shelter will help save a life as well as enrich yours.

Finding the Perfect Puppy

BREEDERS

To find a reputable breeder in your area, start off by contacting the American Kennel Club's (AKC) breeder referral service at 900-407-PUPS. Information provided includes the name and phone number of the national breeder referral contact and, if available, a local contact for the breed you're interested in.

For those with Internet access, go to the website www.akc.org/breeds/groups/index.cfm. Here you'll find that each breed falls under a group heading—Sporting, Hounds, Working, Terriers, Toys, Non-Sporting, and Herding. By clicking on the appropriate group, you'll find a breed's parent club with the appropriate contact information.

Another way to find a breeder is by going to local dog shows or canine sporting events where you'll be able to talk to dog lovers and enthusiasts who can point you in the right direction.

Once you've gotten names of several breeders, you'll need to separate the good from the bad. Picking the right breeder is just as important as picking the right breed. When looking for a breeder, keep in mind that a responsible breeder will have all of the following qualities:

1. He has the puppy's welfare first and foremost in his mind. That means you'll be asked a lot of questions to make sure you'll provide a good home and be a responsible owner. Avoid breeders who are only interested in your money. If this happens don't just walk away—run!

2. He will spend time educating you about the breed. This means talking about the advantages and disadvantages of the breed that you are interested in.

Attending local dog shows or canine sporting events is a good way to find a reputable breeder. It's also an opportunity to talk to other people that own the breed of your choice.

3. He won't hesitate to give names of others who have purchased puppies from him.

4. He does not breed solely to make money. This is a hobby and a true calling, not a source of income. Most breeders have so much money invested in the puppies and their care that they struggle to break even. His or her goal as a breeder should be to improve the breed. One of the puppies is usually kept from the litter to continue this effort.

5. He only sells healthy animals and guarantees them for a reasonable length of time after the sale. Puppies should be tested to certify that their hips, eyes, and ears are free of disease. Which test is performed depends on the breed. Vaccinations should be up-to-date. Records of all veterinary testing and treatment should be made available to you in writing. Avoid breeders that won't refund money or replace a puppy if health problems arise.

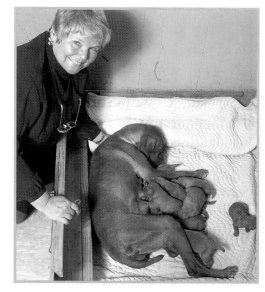

A responsible breeder will only sell healthy puppies complete with a guarantee and will be willing to show you the environment in which the pups were raised.

6. He shows you the environment in which the puppy was raised. It should be clean, secure, and well maintained.

7. He shows you the puppy's mother (dam) and, if on the premises, the father (sire). By observing the dam and sire, you'll have a good idea of what the puppy will be like as an adult. This ranges from coat type to size to temperament.

8. He helps the buyer evaluate and choose the right puppy.

9. He will take a dog back if you can no longer keep him. Whether that's in eight months or eight years, it doesn't make a difference. Good breeders view the puppies as family and don't want them to end up in the pound or roaming the streets homeless. Avoid breeders who won't take back a puppy if for some reason it doesn't work out.

10. After the sale, a good breeder will stay in touch on a regular basis to make sure things are going well and to give you advice, if needed. The breeder is your best source of information over the next 10 to 15 years, which is why it's important to find someone you'll get along with and feel comfortable talking to. If you're not satisfied with a breeder, don't buy the puppy.

Show Dog Versus Pet
For each breed, there is a written description called a breed standard, which explains how the breed should look, move, and act. Breeders strive to produce dogs that closely conform to this standard of perfection. Puppies that come close to the ideal are deemed "show quality." If they have faults, they are referred to as

If you plan to show your dog, make sure that he adheres to the breed standard, which explains how the breed should look, move, and act.

FINDING THE PERFECT PUPPY

"pet quality." The breeder can explain why one puppy is deemed pet and another show. It could be something as simple as he doesn't hold his tail correctly.

Keep in mind, however that there is nothing wrong with pet-quality puppies. They just won't be able to compete in AKC shows successfully. They can still be used in obedience, tracking, field work, or any other activity where physical features are not important. Pet-quality puppies are still good looking, healthy, and best of all, sold for less money than show puppies.

CONTRACTS

Buying a puppy is a major purchase and requires you to sign a contract. Contracts vary from breeder to breeder, so make sure you read it thoroughly. If you don't have to sign a contract, don't purchase the puppy.

Most contracts will have a spay/neuter clause to make sure that a puppy is not bred irresponsibly The AKC registration form (blue slip) can be withheld from you until proof of sterility by a veterinarian is given to the breeder. At that point, the blue slip is turned over to the new owner.

Contracts should also have a 48-hour health guarantee. This gives you enough time to take the puppy to a veterinarian for a checkup. If the puppy ends up not being healthy, you can bring him back to the breeder for a full refund or a new puppy.

LEMON LAWS

Many states have lemon laws that allow you to return a puppy if he becomes ill or physically unfit within a fixed time from the date of purchase. These laws differ from state to state. Some laws make the seller compensate a portion of the veterinarian bills incurred; others cover hereditary conditions over a period of time ranging anywhere from ten days to one year. Such laws, however, provide no real protection against the problems that surface later in a dog's life. That's why it's important to do your homework ahead of time and find a reputable breeder that cares about producing healthy animals.

AKC PAPERS

To register an eligible dog with the AKC, a breeder must furnish one of the following pieces of information listed below. If a seller will not provide this information, do not buy the puppy.

1. AKC Registration Application: This form (known as the blue slip) must be filled out and submitted to the AKC along with the proper fee. You will then receive a registration certificate, which identifies the dog by breed, sex, registered name, and individual registration number. It also shows the name of the breeder, the owner of the dog, and the sire and dam.

If the limited registration box on the application is checked, any offspring of the dog cannot be registered with the AKC. This means a puppy has a trait that the breeder does not want to see passed along. In no way does this mean that the animal is defective. Remember that responsible breeders strive for perfection, and this animal simply does not meet that description but will still make a great pet.

A good breeder is dedicated to producing healthy, sound animals that closely match the breed standard and cares about the welfare of his or her dogs.

2. AKC Registration Certificate: If a dog has already been registered, the seller must furnish you with a registration certificate. Complete the reverse side to indicate transfer.

3. A written bill of sale, which should include the following: breed, sex, coat color, date of birth, registration number, and registered names of sire and dam, as well as name, street, and mailing address of the breeder.

The American Kennel Club has over 15,000 events each year. If you want your puppy to participate in any of these competitions—shows, obedience, or field trials—he must be registered.

However, the AKC is a registry body—that's all. An AKC certificate in no way means that an animal is healthy or sound. That's why it's important to find a reputable breeder that is producing animals that closely match the breed standard, which is a written description of the ideal dog. Every breed recognized by the AKC (over 140) has a national specialty club responsible for this written breed standard. Unfortunately, some people have no concern for highstandards when breeding. Consequently, over several generations, the animals end up having health or temperament problems.

BREED RESCUE GROUPS

If you're interested in a purebred, consider giving a rescue dog a second chance. Breed rescue organizations are made up of people who deeply care about their breed. They take in stray, abandoned, relinquished, and/or impounded purebreds and provide them with foster care until a new home can be found. Unlike city shelters or humane societies, many rescue groups don't have the funds to run a facility, so the dogs are cared for at the homes of volunteers. Rescue workers carefully screen prospective owners in order to make the best match between a dog and an adoptive family. Sometimes this includes follow-up inquiries and visits. The adoption fee is usually less than the cost of buying a puppy from a breeder. Before adopting, find out if the group is reputable by talking to others who have adopted from the organization.

To find a breed rescue group in your area, contact the AKC's Breeder Referral service at 900-407-7877. For a free listing, go to the National Breed Rescue Network's website at www.akc.org/breeds/rescue.cfm.

SHELTERS

If you're not interested in showing your dog, a shelter is the best place to find a new companion. From mixed breeds to purebreds, you'll find just about every shape, size, and color imaginable.

But don't rush into adopting the first big-eyed pup you see. Just as you would look for a reputable breeder, the same holds true in selecting a shelter.

Adopt a dog from a shelter and gain a loyal and loving canine companion in need of a good home. However, before you do so, talk to others who have adopted from the organization and make sure the facilities are clean and run well and that the puppies are healthy.

Talk to others who have adopted from the organization and find out about their experiences. Was the staff helpful and nice? Was the animal healthy? If he was sick, did the shelter pay the medical bills or replace the puppy?

Make a visit to the shelter during business hours. As you walk through the facility, it should be clean and well maintained. Don't be frightened if you hear a lot of barking—this is normal. The dogs are just excited to see visitors and want to be the first to say, "Hi." Be assured that after several minutes, they'll calm down.

While you're there, talk to someone on staff and let them know what you're looking for in a puppy. They can provide vital information about each animal, such as why he was turned in, if he has had any training, and about his personality. The only thing they won't be able to tell you is how big a mixed breed will grow—at best, it's a guess.

If you're looking specifically for a purebred puppy, let the shelter staff know. Many organizations will keep your name and phone number so they can contact you if that particular breed comes in.

While you're there, also inquire if there's a health guarantee. Ask if the puppies are up-to-date with their vaccinations and what the spay/neuter policy is. Some shelters require that a deposit is given on unaltered animals at the time of adoption. The deposit is then refunded once you provide proof of sterilization from a veterinarian. Others sterilize puppies before adopting them out. That means you may have to wait several days before taking your new pet home so that the surgery can be done.

Also, find out if the shelter will take the animal back if the adoption isn't suitable—no matter what the reason. Most shelters will—whether it's in five days

Puppies are very vulnerable to outside diseases. It's important that your puppy is up-to-date with his vaccinations.

Cost, inadequate facilities, and lack of time are just some of the reasons why puppies end up in shelters, so be sure that you can provide all of these things before purchasing a pet.

or five years.

The shelter will also ask you a few questions or require you to fill out an application. This screening process is to make sure that their animals end up in good homes. They'll want to know if you have a fenced-in yard, if you own any other pets, and if you are aware of the special care puppies require.

Many people think there's something "wrong" with animals found at shelters—there's not. Most end up behind bars because their owners didn't consider the work and the cost involved. Consequently, the animals suffer for it.

To gain insight into why some animals end up in shelters, a study was recently conducted by the National Council on Pet Population. Researchers visited 12 animal shelters for 1 year and interviewed owners relinquishing their pets. The top ten reasons for giving up their pets are as follows: moving, landlord did not allow pet, too many animals in household, cost, personal problems, inadequate facilities, no homes available for littermates, no time to spend with pet, illness, and biting.

The study also found that about 47 percent of surrendered dogs were between 5 months and 3 years of age. Dogs acquired from friends were relinquished in higher numbers (31.4 percent) than from any other source, and about 95 percent had not received any obedience training.

Interestingly, about 25 humane societies nationwide have installed cameras in their kennels, which allow potential adopters to view pets 24 hours a day. You must go in person, however, to adopt. Fort Lauderdale-based Internet Global Communications created the Puppy Cam site (www.thepuppycam.com) and hopes to have 400 shelters on the network in the near future.

FINDING THE ONE

If you find a puppy that catches your eye, take time to get to know him. Go for a walk around the grounds or bring him to a quiet area to play. Even though it's tempting, try not to make a decision that day. Wait at least 24 hours. Remember that this decision will affect at least the next 12 years of your life.

If you don't find the perfect puppy on your first visit to a shelter, don't get discouraged. It could take weeks—even months. New animals are turned in daily, so weekly visits are a good idea.

SIGNS OF HEALTH

Whether you buy from a breeder or adopt at a shelter, you'll want to make sure that the puppy is healthy. Look for the following requirements:

—A puppy should be of a proper weight. A bloated belly could mean that he has worms or a too-thin puppy could mean that he's malnourished.

—His ears should look clean, pink, and odor-free.

—His eyes should be clear and bright.

—He should have white teeth and pink gums.

—His coat should be soft, shiny, and free of fleas.

—There should be no blood stains under the tail or signs of diarrhea.

There are plenty of places to get a puppy but there are also a few places to avoid. Never purchase a puppy at a pet store or from a backyard breeder. These animals usually come from puppy mills, which are large-scale breeding

Signs of good health include clean, pink ears, clear, bright eyes, and a soft, shiny coat free of fleas. These baby Schipperkes are the perfect examples of good health.

Although cuddly and furry puppies are often hard to resist, don't select the first one that you fall in love with. Wait at least 24 hours before deciding if that is the right puppy for you.

FINDING THE PERFECT PUPPY

operations that have little regard for producing healthy animals with good temperaments. Reputable breeders never sell to pet stores because they want to screen potential owners to make sure that the puppies go to good homes. Conversely, pet stores employees never ask any questions—except will that be Visa, Master Card, or personal check?

Animals sold in pet stores are never screened for genetic defects, which can lead to problems down the road that could cost you hundreds, if not thousands, of dollars in medical bills. Another problem is that the puppies are often offered limited opportunities for socialization, exercise, and affection, which are necessities during this critical point in their development.

Over recent years, however, more and more pet stores have started to see the light. Instead of selling ill-tempered and sickly animals, they offer to adopt out animals from local humane societies or shelters. This is especially good for people who can't bring themselves to visit a shelter because it's too sad. Adoptions are usually held over the weekends during store hours.

Just about every newspaper in the country has classified ads selling animals. These are usually put in by backyard breeders, which means that they breed the family Doberman to their neighbor's Doberman in order to make a few extra bucks. They have no concern for genetics, bloodlines, or breed improvement. Their prices are at the low end of the range so that they can sell puppies fast, and there are no health guarantees or genetic testing done. Worse yet, if you can't keep the puppy for some reason or if a problem develops—good luck! You're on your own.

PICK OF THE LITTER

Choosing just one puppy from a litter is tough. They will all look so cute and cuddly, you'll be tempted to take them all home! Here's where your hard work in finding the right breeder pays off. Think of him as a matchmaker. He'll be able to tell you which puppy is right for you based on both your personalities. If you're a soft spoken, easygoing type of person, for example, the most aggressive puppy is not for you. This bossy pup will end up telling you what to do, instead of the other way around. Housebreaking and obedience training will be extremely difficult, if not impossible, to accomplish. The same applies if you have a loud, boisterous household with energetic children. You will not want a shy, nervous, or easily frightened pup. He may even turn into a fear biter.

In order to match the right puppy with the right owner, a temperament test can be done. Some breeders wouldn't dream of selling their puppies without performing this type of test. Others feel it's not necessary because they spend enough time with the litter to know each pup's personality. If you feel that a temperament test will help you pick out your perfect pal, try the Puppy Aptitude Test, developed by Jack and Wendy Volhard, owners of Top Dog Training School in Phoenix, New York (reprinted here with permission). It's a little time-consuming but easy to do. Before you begin, though, you'll need to enlist some help, as well as go over the following ground rules:

1. The testing should be done in a location unfamiliar to the puppies, such as a 10-foot square room in the house that the puppies have not been in previously.

Choosing one puppy out of an entire litter can be a difficult choice. Your breeder can help you pick the right puppy to fit your personality and lifestyle.

Make sure that your puppy is fed and well rested before conducting a temperament test.

2. The puppies should be tested one at a time.

3. Besides the scorer and tester, no other dogs or people should be allowed in the testing area.

4. The puppies should not know the tester.

5. The scorer should not be the person interested in selling you the puppy. He should be a disinterested third party.

6. The scorer should be positioned inside the room where he can observe a puppy's response without moving.

7. The puppies should be tested before they are fed.

8. The puppies should be tested when they are their liveliest.

9. You should not test a puppy that is not feeling well.

10. Puppies should not be tested the day of or the day after being vaccinated.

11. The first response that the puppy displays will be the one that counts.

12. During the test, watch if the puppy's tail is up or down. This will make a difference later on in the scoring.

The ideal age to test a puppy is at 49 days of age when he is neurologically complete and has the brain of an adult. If the test is performed after the 49th day, the Volhards say that the puppy's response will be tainted by prior learning. Each of the following tests must be done in the order listed.

1. Social Attraction: The owner or caretaker of the puppy places him in the test area about four feet from the tester and then leaves. The tester kneels down and coaxes the puppy to come to him by gently clapping his hands and calling. The tester must coax the puppy in the opposite direction from where he entered the test area. (Hint: Lean backward, sitting on your heels instead of leaning forward toward the puppy. Keep your hands close to your body when encouraging the puppy to come instead of trying to reach for him.)

2. Following: The tester stands up and slowly walks away, encouraging the puppy to follow. (Hint: Make sure the puppy sees you walk away. Get the puppy to focus on you by lightly clapping your hands and using verbal encouragement. Do not lean over the puppy.)

3. Restraint: The tester crouches down and gently rolls the puppy on his back, holding him there for 30 seconds. (Hint: Hold the puppy down without applying too much pressure. The object is not to keep him on his back but to test his response to being placed in that position.)

4. Social Dominance: While the puppy is either standing or sitting, crouch down and gently stroke him from head to tail. See if he'll lick your face (an indication of a forgiving nature). Continue stroking him until you see a behavior you can score. (Hint: When crouching next to the puppy, avoid leaning or hovering over him. The puppy should be at your side and both of you facing the same direction.)

5. Elevation Dominance: The tester cradles the puppy with both hands, supporting him under the chest. The tester then gently lifts the puppy two feet off the ground and holds him there for 30 seconds.

Retrieving is one of the elements of the Puppy Aptitude Test. The desired response is for your dog to retrieve the object and return it to the tester with little or no difficulty.

6. Retrieving: The tester crouches beside the puppy and tries to get his attention with a crumpled piece of paper. When the puppy shows some interest, the tester throws the paper no more than four feet in front of the puppy and encourages him to retrieve it.

7. Touch Sensitivity: The tester locates the webbing of one of the puppy's front paws and presses it lightly between his index finger and thumb. The tester gradually increases pressure while counting to ten but stops if the puppy pulls away or shows signs of discomfort.

8. Sound Sensitivity: The puppy is placed in the center of the test area and an assistant stationed at the perimeter makes a sharp noise, such as banging a spoon on the bottom of a metal pan.

9. Sight Sensitivity: The puppy is placed in the center of the testing area. The tester ties a string around a bath towel and jerks it across the floor, two feet away from the puppy.

10. Stability: An umbrella is opened about five feet from the puppy and gently placed on the ground.

Scoring

Test 1. Social Attraction
   Response: Came readily, tail up, jumped, bit at hands/Score: 1
   Response: Came readily, tail up, pawed, licked at hands/Score: 2
   Response: Came readily, tail up/Score: 3
   Response: Came readily, tail down/Score: 4
   Response: Came hesitantly, tail down/Score: 5
   Response: Didn't come at all/Score: 6

Test 2. Following
   Response: Followed readily, tail up, got underfoot, bit at feet/Score: 1
   Response: Followed readily, tail up, got underfoot/Score: 2
   Response: Followed readily, tail up/Score: 3
   Response: Followed readily, tail down/Score: 4
   Response: Followed hesitantly, tail down/Score: 5
   Response: Did not follow or went away/Score: 6

Test 3. Restraint
   Response: Struggled fiercely, flailed, bit/Score: 1
   Response: Struggled fiercely, flailed/Score: 2
   Response: Settled, struggled, settled with some eye contact/Score: 3
   Response: Struggled, then settled/Score: 4
   Response: No struggle/Score: 5
   Response: No struggle, strained to avoid eye contact/Score: 6

Test 4. Social Dominance
   Response: Jumped, pawed, bit, growled/Score: 1
   Response: Jumped, pawed/Score: 2
   Response: Cuddled up to tester and tried to lick face/Score: 3
   Response: Squirmed, licked at hands/Score: 4
   Response: Rolled over, licked at hands/Score: 5
   Response: Went away and stayed away/Score: 6

Test 5. Elevation Dominance
   Response: Struggled fiercely, tried to bite/Score: 1
   Response: Struggled fiercely/Score: 2
   Response: Struggled, settled, struggled, settled/Score: 3
   Response: No struggle, relaxed/Score: 4
   Response: No struggle, body stiff/Score: 5
   Response: No struggle, froze/Score: 6

Test 6. Retrieving
    Response: Chased object, picked it up, and ran away/Score: 1
    Response: Chased object, stood over it, and did not return/Score: 2
    Response: Chased object, picked it up, and returned with it to tester/Score: 3
    Response: Chased object and returned without it to tester/Score: 4
    Response: Started to chase object, lost interest/Score: 5
    Response: Does not chase object/Score: 6

Test 7. Touch Sensitivity
    Response: 8 - 10 count before response/Score: 1
    Response: 6 - 8 count before response/Score: 2
    Response: 5 - 6 count before response/Score: 3
    Response: 3 - 5 count before response/Score: 4
    Response: 2 - 3 count before response/Score: 5
    Response: 1-2 count before response/Score: 6

Test 8. Sound Sensitivity
    Response: Listened, located sound, and ran toward it barking/Score: 1
    Response: Listened, located sound, and walked slowly toward it/Score: 2
    Response: Listened, located sound, and showed curiosity/Score: 3
    Response: Listened and located sound/Score: 4
    Response: Cringed, backed off, and hid behind tester/Score: 5
    Response: Ignored sound and showed no curiosity/Score: 6

Test 9. Sight Sensitivity
    Response: Looked, attacked, and bit object/Score: 1
    Response: Looked, put feet on object, and put mouth on it/Score: 2
    Response: Looked with curiosity and attempted to investigate, tail up/Score: 3
    Response: Looked with curiosity, tail down/Score: 4
    Response: Ran away or hid behind tester/Score: 5
    Response: Hid behind tester/Score: 6

Test 10. Stability
    Response: Looked and ran to the umbrella, mouthing or biting it/Score: 1
    Response: Looked and walked to the umbrella, smelling it cautiously/Score: 2
    Response: Looked and went to investigate/Score: 3
    Response: Sat and looked but did not move toward the umbrella/Score: 3
    Response: Showed little or no interest/Score: 4
    Response: Ran away from the umbrella/Score: 5
    Response: Showed no interest/Score: 6

WHAT THE SCORE MEANS

For the first-time owner, look for a puppy with quite a few 3's and 4's in his score. Don't worry about the score on touch sensitivity, because you can compensate for that with the right training equipment. Avoid the puppy with a score of 1 on the Restraint and Elevation tests. This puppy will be too much for the first-time owner. Also, stay away from the puppy that scores a lot of 1's and 2's—he has leadership aspirations and may be difficult to manage. This puppy needs an experienced home and is not good with children.

Mostly 1's—This puppy has a strong desire to be pack leader and is not shy about bucking for a promotion. He always has a predisposition to be aggressive with people and other dogs and will bite. He should only be placed into a very experienced home where he will be trained on a regular basis.

Mostly 2's—This puppy also has leadership aspirations. He may be hard to manage and has the capacity to bite. He has lots of self-confidence and should not be placed into an inexperienced home. He may be too unruly to be good with children, elderly people, or other animals. He needs a strict schedule, loads of exercise, and lots of training. This puppy has the potential to be a great show dog with someone who understands dog behavior.

Mostly 3's—This puppy can be a high-energy dog and may need lots of exercise. He will be good with people and other animals but can be a bit of a handful to live with. He needs training but learns quickly. This is a great dog for second-time owners.

Mostly 4's—This dog makes a perfect pet and is the best choice for first-time owners. He'll rarely buck for a promotion in the family. He is easy to train and rather quiet. He will be good with elderly people and children but may need protection from the kids. Choose this pup, take him to obedience classes, and you'll have a star without having to do too much work!

Mostly 5's—This puppy is fearful, shy, and needs special handling. He'll run away at the slightest stress in his life. Strange people, strange places, different floor or ground surfaces may upset him, and he will often be afraid of loud noises and terrified of thunderstorms. When you greet him upon your return, he may submissively urinate. He needs a very special home where the environment doesn't change too much and there are no children. He would be best for a quiet, elderly couple; however, if cornered and cannot get away, he may have the tendency to bite.

Mostly 6's—This puppy is fiercely independent. He doesn't need you or other people, and doesn't care if he's trained or not. He will be unlikely to bond to you, because he feels that he doesn't need you. Do not take this puppy and think that you can change him into a lovable bundle—you can't, so leave well enough alone.

By choosing a healthy, well-socialized puppy with the right temperament for your situation and by getting the puppy from a reputable source, you are ensuring that you, your family, and your puppy all get off on the right paw together.

The right pet can enrich your life in many ways. Choose carefully to ensure a long and happy life together for both dog and owner.

Getting Prepared

Before bringing your puppy home, you'll need to buy a few supplies from the following shopping list:

DISHES

Buy one dish for food and a slightly larger one for water. Ceramic or heavy stainless steel dishes are usually your best bet because they won't tip over easily or slide around on the floor while your puppy is trying to eat. For sanitary reasons, bowls should be washed in warm, soapy water after every meal or placed in the dishwasher.

FOOD

Find out what brand the breeder or shelter fed your puppy. It's a good idea to stick with the same brand until your puppy is housetrained, because a sudden change in diet can cause diarrhea.

COLLAR

A proper fit is important—you don't want it to be too tight or too loose. To figure out what size collar to buy, measure around your puppy's neck, close to his

Stainless steel dishes are sturdy and easy to clean. Bowls should always be washed in warm, soapy water after every meal.

Your puppy will greatly appreciate having a soft, comfortable bed to sleep in. Choose one that will fit him as an adult and that is easy to clean.

shoulders, then add two inches. As he grows, you'll need to adjust the collar from time to time so that it doesn't get too tight. You should be able to fit two fingers underneath the collar at all times.

IDENTIFICATION TAG

More than 10 million pets are lost each year, but few are ever reunited with their owners. Identification tags are your best hope of getting your puppy back if he becomes lost. Many pet supply stores have machines that will engrave a custom tag in just minutes. If you don't like the sound of clanging tags, buy a collar with a brass nameplate.

BED

There are all shapes, sizes, and colors to choose from. Pick one that will accommodate your puppy once he's fully grown. A removable, machine-washable cover will make cleaning easy.

GROOMING TOOLS

Even if you plan on taking your puppy to a groomer, you'll still need to do some work in between appointments. For long-haired breeds, buy a soft slicker brush and metal comb. A pin brush works well for short coats. You'll also need shampoo that won't irritate eyes and an ear cleaner.

TOYS

Buy chew toys that can't be torn apart or easily swallowed. Nylon or hard rubber bones are safe choices for teething puppies.

Keeping your puppy off of freshly fertilized lawns will help prevent him from becoming sick.

PUPPY PROOFING

Curious pups love to explore, and that usually means one thing—trouble. Before bringing your puppy home, secure household items that can be easily tipped over. A good puppy-proofing rule to follow is to keep everything up high and out of paw's reach. Also, consider buying a baby gate to block off areas your puppy isn't allowed to enter. Here are a few tips:

—Don't leave shoes, purses, or clothing lying around unless you want to start a new trend—apparel and accessories accented with teeth marks. Get into a habit of keeping closet doors shut.

—To prevent electrocution keep cords out of reach and, if possible, unplugged. For appliances or lamps that need to stay plugged in, buy a commercial chew-proof guard.

—Fence in your pool or spa to prevent your puppy from falling in and drowning. If you can't afford to fence in your pool or spa, teach your puppy how to swim and where the steps are so he can get out.

—Put childproof latches on cabinets and drawers containing poisonous products, like medication or cleaning supplies.

—Don't allow your puppy in the garage. If antifreeze leaks from your car and your puppy laps up the sweet tasting liquid, it can kill him.

—Keep your puppy off freshly fertilized lawns. The chemicals can either burn the pads of his feet or make him sick if he licks his paws afterward.

Children and Dog Ownership

A ll kids can benefit from having a pet in the house. It helps build self-esteem, teaches responsibility, and provides companionship. However, children need to be taught that there's more to owning a puppy than just providing plenty of hugs and kisses. It requires a lot of work. A dog must be fed, walked, and cleaned up after every day. While parents shouldn't expect their children to do all the work, they can expect them to take an active role in the day-to-day pet care. The kinds of tasks kids are capable of handling depends on how old they are. Children under 12 don't have the physical or mental ability to care for a dog on their own and should only be viewed as helpers.

"Up until that age a pet is a wonderful addition to the family, but parents need to understand that it's a family pet, not the child's pet," says Elizabeth Pantley, author of Perfecting Parenting and Kid Cooperation. "Mom and dad will be doing the majority of care."

A six-year-old child, for example, can have the "job" of feeding the puppy, but parents will have to give daily reminders and pitch in frequently. Once a child is ten years old, he can graduate from a helper to an official owner by taking a more active role in daily pet-care responsibilities. Parents at this point should act as

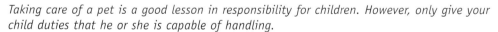

Taking care of a pet is a good lesson in responsibility for children. However, only give your child duties that he or she is capable of handling.

Having a pet can help build a child's self-esteem, teach responsibility, and provide companionship.

managers by assigning jobs and following up to make sure they get done. One way to do this is by creating a Pet Care Chart, which lists everything on a large poster board that needs to be done on a daily and weekly basis. After each chore, draw a series of boxes for check marks, labeled by days of the week. Hang the poster in a visible place (like the kitchen or your child's bedroom) as a reminder of what needs to be done. After each chore has been completed, have your child check off the appropriate box.

"A Pet Care Chart helps in two ways," says Pantley. "It provides a written "to do" list so chores can easily be remembered and helps develop a routine."

At first, assign just one chore. As your child masters it, add another. In the beginning, don't throw all the work in their lap. It takes about two weeks for a child to master a job and for it to become part of his routine. After a couple of months, the assigned chore will become easier because it's familiar and he'll be able to complete it faster.

If you have more than one child and they get tired of their assigned chore, let them switch after several weeks. Parents should also keep in mind the Pet Care Chart is not etched in stone. If a child has a busy schedule one week and is running off to baseball or soccer games, it's okay to pitch in and help out.

Besides displaying a chart, another way to help children remember their daily pet-care responsibilities is to tie the chore to other daily rituals. For example, make it your child's chore to feed the dog after dinner. This way it's connected to something he does every day and will be easier to remember.

But what if your child still forgets to do his chores?

"Use logical consequences," explains Pantley, who is the mother of three. "Let your child know that if his chores are not done when he leaves for school you will do them for him. Then, when he comes home from school, he can do a few of your chores." For example, if the dog's food and water dishes are empty after your child leaves for the day, you fill them. Then when your child returns home from school, have him take over your chore of folding the laundry.

Parents should never threaten to get rid of the puppy if chores are not done. It sends a negative message that you don't care about the dog, and that he's not important to the family. Instead let your children know why it's important for them to pitch in. Tell them how their puppy relies on them for care and how he looks forward to them coming home from school so they can play together. Explain to them that in order for the puppy to grow up healthy and strong, he needs to eat, go for walks, and have a clean place to go to the potty.

"Kids like to be grown up, independent, and mature," says Pantley. "By looking at it this way, they feel very important, like—wow, my dog is counting on me! Once they see their job as being really important to the dog, they'll take more interest in that."

TEACHING CHILDREN HOW TO TREAT PETS

Children don't automatically know right from wrong; it's up to you to show them. Following are a few things to go over with your child before bringing home your puppy.

Let your child take an active role in the responsibilities of daily pet care. Having a chart can help him or her keep track of daily chores.

—Treat animals gently. Children are curious and sometimes do things just to see what happens. That can mean yanking on tails, pulling at ears, and poking at eyes. Show your children what parts they can touch and explain that yanking, pulling, and poking hurts the puppy. Many young children, though well meaning, have a tendency to pet roughly. Sit down with your children and show them how to gently stroke the puppy.

—Don't allow children younger than ten years of age to pick up a puppy. Instead, have your child sit on the floor and place the puppy in his or her lap. This way they can enjoy holding the puppy and if he squirms out of your child's arms, he won't fall and get hurt.

—Tell your children not to disturb the puppy while he's sleeping, eating, or playing with a favorite toy. These are times when dogs don't like to be bothered and, if pestered, may try and bite.

—Don't allow children and pets to share snacks. By giving a puppy bits and pieces of food, it teaches him that begging pays off, and he'll end up constantly bothering the family during meals. Human food also disrupts a dog's sensitive digestive system and can cause an upset stomach or diarrhea.

—Don't let children give the puppy small objects or toys, which can easily be swallowed.

—When your child's friends come over to play, supervise the visit. Some children haven't been taught how to treat pets properly. They might think it's funny to chase, hit, or throw things at the puppy. Remember, the sweetest pup will bite if provoked, so if your young guests can't be trusted, lock the puppy in a safe place until they leave.

Just as children need to be taught how to treat puppies, puppies need to be taught how to act around children. One of the main things puppies need to learn is not to jump up on the kids, which can knock them over or scratch them. The best way to instill manners in your puppy is by enrolling him in an obedience

A gentle and well-mannered puppy is a pleasure to have around, especially when you have children. Enrolling your puppy in an obedience class will instill good manners and teach him the basic commands.

class where he'll learn basic commands, such as sit, stay, down, and come, and have your children participate in the training with you.

PREVENTING DOG BITES

More than half of all children aged 12 and younger in the United States will be bitten by a dog. Most of these bites are from a neighbor's, friend's, or even the family's dog. To prevent your child from becoming a victim, here are a few rules to go over with him or her:

—Don't approach strange dogs.

—Ask permission from a dog's owners before petting him. If they say it's okay to pet their dog, approach him from the front, hold out your closed fist for him to sniff, and speak softly to him.

—Never leave young children alone with a dog—even the family pet.

—Stay away from a dog when his ears are back, legs are stiff, tail is up, or the hair on his back is standing up.

—When a dog growls, it means to stay away.

—Never approach a barking dog—even if his tail is wagging.

—Don't bother a dog when he is eating or sleeping.

—Don't tease a dog.

—Don't run past a dog. Dogs instinctively love to chase and catch things.

—If a strange dog approaches—stay still. Remain calm and avoid eye contact, which dogs perceive as threatening. In most cases, the dog will go away when he determines you're not a threat. If the dog knocks you down, curl into a ball, and place your hands over your head and neck.

Nutrition and Diet

Providing a high-quality diet is essential for fast-growing puppies. In human terms, a dog grows as much in the first year as a human does in the first 14 years of life. That's why your puppy needs a diet dense in calories to keep up with this fast-paced growth.

Selecting the right brand to meet your puppy's nutritional needs isn't difficult. Look for a commercial brand formulated for growth. It should state this clearly on the bag as well as have the Association of American Feed Control Officials statement declaring that the food provides "complete and balanced nutrition for growth." AAFCO tests food to ensure that it meets certain nutritional standards. If it doesn't have the AAFCO statement, don't buy it.

If you purchased your puppy from a breeder, the decision on what brand to buy is easy—get the same one he fed. This will prevent your puppy from having an upset stomach or diarrhea, which can be caused by a sudden change in diet. Because your puppy will be a little nervous at first while adjusting to his new home, it's best to stick with this brand for awhile. If you decide to switch brands later on, gradually mix increasing amounts of the new food with decreasing proportions of the old over several days.

Also, find out from the breeder how much was fed and at what times. Try to stick with this schedule until your puppy gets adjusted to his new home. Dogs are creatures of habit and feel more comfortable with familiar routines.

If you don't know your puppy's prior feeding schedule, start off by following the suggested guidelines on the label. Remember that these are just suggestions, and you'll probably have to increase or decrease the amount fed based on your puppy's breed and activity level. Ask your veterinarian for advice.

Because puppies have tiny tummies, they'll need to be fed small portions several times a day. Provide four meals a day (morning, midday, mid-afternoon, and an hour before bedtime) until they are 16 weeks old. Then reduce to three meals a day until they reach eight months of age. When your puppy nears adulthood, which can be anywhere from six months to two years depending on

Your breeder should have started your puppy on the road to good nutrition. Find out what brand of food was given, the amount, and at what times during the day before taking the puppy home.

Feed your puppy a diet appropriate for his age and weight. Larger breeds need a special diet that will help control their growth rate.

the breed, feed him twice a day and change to a diet formulated for maintenance.

SPECIAL DIET

If you own a large-or giant-breed puppy, consider buying a specially formulated food to control their growth rate. These breeds, whose adult weight will be greater than 60 pounds, tend to suffer from skeletal abnormalities like hip dysplasia if they grow and gain weight too fast. Special diets, which have been reduced in total energy, calories, and fat, have been created to control the rate of growth and prevent these debilitating and potentially crippling conditions from developing. The diet won't affect how big your puppy will ultimately become; genetics have already determined that. Most pet supply stores carry large-and giant-breed puppy formulas.

SUPPLEMENTS

By feeding your puppy a good-quality commercial diet, nutritional supplements are not needed. In some cases, in fact, it may even be harmful. Calcium supplements, for example, can upset the delicate balance of mineral absorption and cause a secondary zinc deficiency, which in turn can cause skin diseases and stunt growth. Consult your veterinarian before adding any kind of supplements to your pet's diet.

CANNED, SEMI-MOIST, OR DRY

As long as your puppy is receiving a nutritionally balanced diet, the decision on which type of food to buy comes down to what works best for you.

For busy people that work long hours, a dry formula is a good choice because it can be left in a bowl all day without spoiling. It's the least expensive, and some studies have shown that dry kibble helps to scrape tartar off teeth, which promotes good oral health. The downside is that it's the least tastiest.

Semi-moist food comes in convenient, prepackaged single servings so that owners don't have to bother measuring, but the large amounts of sugar and preservatives added to maintain its freshness without refrigeration are unhealthy.

Canned food is the most expensive and requires more of it to be fed because the energy content is relatively low, especially for large breeds. It's the tastiest of the three but will spoil if left out for more than 30 minutes.

Some owners mix canned and dry food together. This common practice has prompted some manufacturers to include special feeding instructions on the label.

STORAGE

Spoiled food can cause vomiting, diarrhea, and other serious health problems. That's why it's important to store food properly.

Dry food should be kept in a cool, dry, dark place. Make sure to tightly seal any unused portions to prevent air from getting in, which can cause it to spoil. You can find specially designed storage containers with airtight lids at most pet supply stores. These storage containers are also great for preventing pesky bugs from getting into the food. When properly kept, dry food is guaranteed fresh up to 12 months from the date of manufacture.

Unopened canned products can last 18 months from the date of manufacture. Once opened, however, it needs to be refrigerated and used within two days.

Besides proper storage, owners should look for a "best if used by" date on the label to ensure that the product is fresh. More and more manufacturers are adding this important piece of information to their labels.

It's also a good idea when buying pet food to shop at stores that have a high turnover. This way if the product doesn't have an expiration date, you won't be stuck with food that's been sitting on the shelf too long.

TABLE SCRAPS

It's okay to give your dog healthy table scraps from time to time—just don't overdo it. Feeding too many treats throughout the day can create a finicky eater or, worse yet, cause your dog to pack on a few extra pounds. Snacks should comprise less than 10 percent of your dog's daily caloric intake.

Some healthy snacks you and your pooch can share are carrots, broccoli, cauliflower, cooked zucchini, apple slices, raisins, and seedless grapes. Popcorn (without butter), ice cubes—the ultimate low-calorie treat—cooked fish, chicken, or lean beef can also be given. Avoid chicken skin or turkey skin and lunch meats that are high in fat and calories. Hot dogs, ice cream, cookies, cake, and chocolate, which can be extremely toxic, should also be avoided.

BONES

Puppies love to chew on bones. In fact, experts even say it's good for them because it helps scrape tartar off teeth, which promotes good oral health. But turkey, pork, or chicken bones that can easily splinter, causing digestive upsets and intestinal blockage, should be avoided. Knuckle or marrowbones are good choices because they don't break apart easily.

Chewing sessions should be closely monitored. If your puppy starts to eat the bone, immediately take it away.

HOMEMADE DIETS

The field seems to be evenly divided over this somewhat controversial issue. Opponents say that home-cooked meals don't provide all the necessary nutrients that your pet needs to stay healthy. Besides, shopping for ingredients and cooking is more of a hassle than simply ripping open a bag of kibble.

But those in favor of homemade diets say that it's worth the extra effort. They

Spoiled food can cause vomiting, diarrhea, and other health complications in your dog. Be aware of how long your dog's food is left out.

NUTRITION AND DIET

claim that commercial pet foods are filled with moldy grains, rancid animal fat, and contaminated meat. These questionable ingredients are just downright unhealthy, they say, and owners need to take matters into their own hands—and kitchens.

To an extent, both sides are right. If you have the extra time, the money, and the belief that it's healthier for your pet to eat a home-cooked meal, then you should do it. Just make sure you go to a reputable source for a nutritionally balanced recipe. Your veterinarian might be able to suggest a recipe or at least give you information on where to find one. For owners whose lives are extremely busy, you're best sticking with a high-quality commercial diet. Each year, pet food manufacturers spend millions on nutritional research, and despite the critics, many dogs lead happy, healthy lives on store-bought food.

WATER

Your pet can live without food for several days, but just a 15-percent loss in body water can result in death. A big bowl of fresh, clean, drinking water should always be available. Change it every morning and check it throughout the day to make sure it's full.

If your backyard pooch likes to knock over his water dish, try filling a bucket with water then burying it halfway into the ground. Make sure that the bucket is in an area that stays shady all day, otherwise the sun will make the water too hot to drink. To help keep the water cool during the hot summer months, fill the bucket with equal amounts of ice and water. As the ice melts, it provides a constant source of cool, drinking water.

Dogs need a constant supply of fresh, clean water. If your dog has a tendency to knock over his water bowl, try using a sturdy bucket.

Grooming

PROFESSIONAL GROOMING

There is no state or federal regulations governing the pet grooming industry, so it's up to you to visit several establishments before making an appointment.

"When you walk in the shop, look around and take a deep breath," advises Jeff Reynolds, executive director of the National Dog Groomers Association of America. "You'll know right away whether or not to drop your doggie off there."

The shop should be clean, he says, and the groomer should act and look professional. Also, take note of how the animals on the grooming tables are being handled. Would you want your dog to be handled in the same manner?

If your dog is not used to going to a groomer, avoid using high volume shops. They simply won't have the extra time or patience needed to spend with your dog.

Inquire if the groomer is certified by an industry organization. The National Dog Groomers Association, for example, requires hands-on testing as well as a written exam in order to join. Find out if the groomer attends workshops, seminars, or competitions held throughout the United States. These programs help further a groomer's education and keep him or her current on industry standards and trends. Last, but not least, ask for references.

Daily brushing helps keep your dog's coat in excellent condition, and it is a good way to detect any skin irritations.

DOING IT YOURSELF

Brushing

Daily brushing is an essential part of good grooming. It removes dead hair and skin, as well as helps put natural oils back into the coat. For long-haired breeds, you'll need a soft slicker brush and metal comb. For puppies with short, smooth coats, a pin brush works best.

Always brush in the direction that the coat lies. If you want the hair to stick up and be fluffy, like a Poodle's coat, then brush against the grain.

"Think of the dog as having four sides," says award-winning groomer, Christina Pawlosky, who

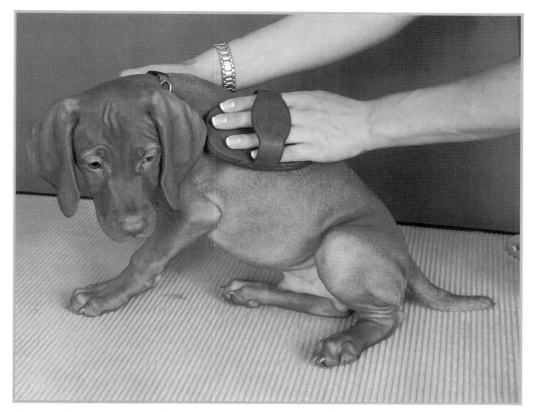

If you notice any abnormalities on your puppy's skin while brushing his coat, such as swelling, scaliness, or changes in pigmentation, consult your veterinarian.

works for Oster grooming products. "You do the inside of the back leg; the outside of the back leg; then the front and the back." Continue this approach for the rest of the body.

Seasonal changes, different stages of life, and certain hormones can all cause hair loss. By sticking to a regular brushing schedule, however, shedding won't pose much of a problem. If dead hair is not removed it can form mats, which can lead to skin problems.

Pawlosky doesn't recommend using scissors to chop out mats, because too many people end up cutting their dog instead of the hair. Instead, use a mat rack, which is a comb with sharp blades on one side. This special tool splits the tangled mass of hair in half and makes it easier to comb out with a slicker brush. If you're planning on giving your puppy a bath, remove all mats before you bathe him. Water tightens the hair, making it difficult to brush out later.

If you notice any redness, swelling, breaks in the skin, scaliness, or changes in pigmentation during regular brushings, consult your veterinarian.

To check your dog's coat for fleas, ticks, and other parasites, use a flea comb (a small, closely spaced comb) once a week. If you get a black, gritty material off your pet, check to see if it's flea dirt by placing the material on a white towel and adding a couple drops of water. If it dissolves and turns a pinkish red, it's dried blood, which means your pet has fleas.

You can also visually check for the small blood-sucking parasites by parting the coat around the abdomen, armpits, and hindquarters.

Ears

It's important to remove wax and dirt buildup on a regular basis in order to prevent ear infections. Ask your veterinarian to recommend a cleaning solution and follow the directions on the label. Only clean the visible areas of the ear—never try and clean the inside portion you can't see.

In general, ears should be cleaned once a month. Breeds with long, floppy ears, like Cocker Spaniels, have to be done more often. Older dogs might also need extra attention. As some dogs age, an oily, dark brown buildup occurs inside their ears. If you notice a disagreeable odor or excessive discharge, consult your veterinarian right away.

Eyes

Some breeds, like Poodles and Bichon Frises, get tear stains near their eyes. This is usually caused by clogged tear ducts. Then, when normal tears spill out, they oxidize and cause a discoloration of the hair. There are specially formulated cleaners that are sold at pet supply stores that can remove stains and return hair to its normal color.

Check your puppy's feet for embedded burrs, twigs, or pebbles after he has been playing outside. If these small objects are not removed, they could cause your dog a great deal of discomfort.

Feet

After your puppy goes for a walk or hike, check in between the pads of his feet for burrs, twigs, or pebbles. If not removed, these small objects can cause a great deal of discomfort.

During the summer, surfaces heat up quickly and can burn tender foot pads. Before venturing out with your best friend, first feel how hot the cement or asphalt is with your hand. Try taking walks during the morning or at dusk when surface temperatures are cooler. As the weather turns cold, another potential problem arises. Salt or other de-icers used on driveways and walkways can irritate and burn. To protect your pet's feet all year, consider buying your puppy the specially made boots for canines that are sold in pet supply stores and catalogues.

Be very gentle when cutting your dog's nails. Cutting into the quick of the nail is painful and will cause bleeding.

Nails

Trimming your dog's nails can be tricky, because each nail has a blood vessel, called the quick, that runs through its center. In light-colored nails, it's usually visible, but in dark-colored nails, it's not. Cutting the quick hurts your dog and causes profuse bleeding. If the quick is cut by accident, applying styptic powder or liquid will help stop the bleeding.

If you don't feel comfortable trimming your puppy's nails, take him to a groomer or veterinarian. Nails should be trimmed every two to three months. You'll know if your puppy's nails are the proper length if they don't touch the ground while your dog is standing.

BATHING

There are no rules on bathing your puppy. Whenever your puppy is dirty or smells, break out the shampoo! Today's formulas are gentler than ever before, which allows owners to bathe their pets more often without worrying about damaging coats. To keep your puppy looking his best, however, you should bathe him at least once a month.

The skin and hair of dogs have a different pH level than humans, so only use shampoos made specifically for pets. Select a shampoo that doesn't contain a lot of ingredients. This will lessen the chance that your puppy will have an adverse reaction to it.

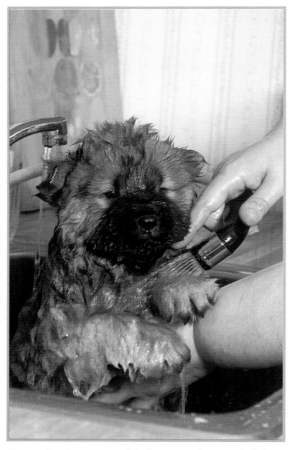

Remember to use a mild shampoo that won't irritate your dog's eyes, as well as a conditioner to help protect the skin and keep the coat manageable.

If your dog doesn't have any skin problems (like dry, itchy skin), buy a mild, pleasant-smelling shampoo that won't irritate eyes. You should also buy a conditioner, which will help seal and protect the skin and leave the coat manageable and healthy.

Before you start drawing the water, make sure that all mats and tangles have been removed, then loosely plug your puppy's ears with cotton so water won't get inside.

If you have a small dog, consider buying a lightweight tub that can be placed on a countertop instead of using a bathtub. This will save you from bending down constantly while bathing. These tubs are sold at pet supply stores or in catalogues. If you have a large-sized dog, he should be bathed in the tub or outside if the weather permits.

When bathing, use lukewarm water. Soak your puppy thoroughly before applying shampoo. If using a flea or tick shampoo, read the directions carefully before applying it to your dog's coat.

Lather up well, working the shampoo into the skin. Completely remove the shampoo by using clean water. (Residue left from shampoos can cause flaking and itching.) To get a constant flow of clean water, connect a sprayer to the faucet or shower head. While rinsing, pour the water in the same direction that the coat lies to prevent tangles and mats.

Now the fun part—drying your puppy. There's nothing more aggravating than chasing a wet dog around the house, so at this point, you might want to enlist some help. Start by towel drying, gently pulling the coat in the direction you want it to lie. Continue patting dry until no water drips. After you get all the excess water out of the coat, you can either let your dog dry naturally or use a hand-held hair dryer on a warm setting. When using a dryer, keep the air constantly flowing over the body on a warm to cool setting. Holding it in one spot for any length of time at too hot a temperature will burn his skin. Once completely dry, brush out your pup's coat one more time.

With a little effort and a lot of patience, you will have a pretty puppy in no time.

Housetraining

With frequent trips outside, a regular feeding schedule, and a lot of patience, your puppy can be housetrained in a few weeks. Start by setting up a regular feeding schedule for your dog. Meals should be served at the same time and place every day. The amount of food given should also be consistent. A handful or bowlful can mean different things to different family members, so break out those measuring cups. Remember that the serving portion listed on the brand's label is for the entire day. To calculate a single portion, divide the suggested amount by how many times a day (two or three) you feed your pet.

Avoid feeding table scraps or changing brands while housetraining, because it can cause an upset stomach or diarrhea. If you must make a switch, do it gradually over a four- to seven-day period by mixing increasing amounts of the new food with decreasing portions of the old.

Meals should only be left out for 30 to 40 minutes and then removed. This will make your puppy's elimination schedule more predictable. Most puppies have to go outside an hour after eating, and very young puppies tend to eliminate 20 or 30 minutes after a meal.

Keeping track of your puppy's defecating and urinating schedule will help prevent accidents. Each time your puppy goes outside and eliminates, mark down the time on a piece of paper. Continue to do this for at least a week. Soon a pattern will develop, and you'll have a good idea of when to take him outside.

Puppies also need to go to the bathroom after they eat, drink, play, chew, or sleep.

Keeping a schedule of when your puppy eliminates will help prevent accidents. Most puppies have to go outside an hour after eating a meal.

Puppies will usually try to communicate to their people when they have to go to the bathroom, either by circling or sniffing at the door or staring at their owner. Very young puppies may need to be picked up and taken outside.

For pups that are ten weeks of age or older, that means five to ten times a day.

When outside, go to the same area. The odor from previous visits will remind him why he's there. After eliminating, immediately praise him by saying, "Good dog." Positive reinforcement speeds along the training process. Sometimes puppies urinate or defecate more than once per outing. After he relieves himself, don't rush back inside. Wait a few more minutes just in case.

If your puppy does not eliminate when he's outside, go back in and wait 15 minutes. Then take him outside again. Keep this up until he finally goes.

Until your dog is fully housebroken, he'll require constant supervision while indoors. One way to do this, says Lisa Aprea, who runs Happy-Dog Training in Boston, Massachusetts, is by using a puppy "umbilical cord." Start by attaching one end of a long leash to your puppy and the other end to you. Now everywhere you go, he goes too. This method helps prevent accidents, because you'll notice signs that your puppy may need to eliminate (such as sniffing the floor, circling, or suddenly trying to run out of sight).

If your puppy eliminates in front of you, firmly and in a low voice say, "No." This will usually make him stop. Then immediately take him outside to finish. With very young puppies, pick them up and bring them outdoors. Once you are outside and he finishes eliminating, praise him warmly.

If the umbilical cord method isn't appealing and you can't keep a close eye on your puppy, use an adjustable, see-through gate to confine him in a room with a hard floor, like the kitchen or bathroom. Now, if an accident happens, it will be easier to clean up.

If you forget to confine your puppy and he makes a mistake inside, don't rub his nose in the mess. Dogs can only associate a reward or punishment with the act that they are performing at the time. He won't understand that a mistake he made 20 minutes ago is now upsetting you.

Messes should be cleaned up right away. Two common mistakes owners make are using diluted vinegar or an ammonia-based cleaner. Vinegar is not effective in removing the smell of urine. In fact, one veterinarian says that some animals are attracted by the smell of vinegar and will go back and urinate over it. Ammonia breaks down to urea, which is a component of urine, so you end up cleaning an area with something that smells like what you're trying to get rid of.

The only way to completely remove the odor is by using an enzyme-based deodorizer, which is available at most pet supply stores. Getting rid of the smell is important because dogs will go back to that same spot to relieve themselves.

Mistakes can be distressful, but keep in mind submissive or excitement urination is totally involuntary. It can be triggered by a number of things, including eye contact, verbal scolding, petting, animated movements, and talking in an excited or loud voice, as well as strangers or visitors. Never scold your puppy for submissive or excitement urination. It will only make the problem worse.

If your puppy is really having trouble with his housetraining, consult your veterinarian. There could be an underlying medical condition, such as internal parasites or a bladder infection, that is hindering successful training. Also, don't expect puppies that are under 14 weeks of age to be housebroken completely, because they don't have full muscle control yet.

Paper train your dog if you are unable to let him out to relieve himself during the day.

PAPER TRAINING

This method is good for elderly or handicapped owners, people who work long hours, or people who live in high-rise apartment buildings. It also works best for small dogs.

When you paper train your pet, you teach him to relieve himself on thick layers of newspaper indoors. As with housebreaking, a regular feeding schedule, time limits on meals, and constant supervision are extremely important.

The first step in paper training is to pick a spot in the house where your dog will be allowed to eliminate. The area should be about three square feet and away from where he sleeps and eats. Layer this area with newspaper or put a shallow pan filled with sod. Take your puppy to this location after every meal, as well as first thing in the morning and right before bedtime. If he shows signs that he has to eliminate, take him to this spot. Each time he relieves himself in the right place, praise him warmly.

Once you've established an area, don't change it. This will only confuse your puppy. Over the next several weeks, with a lot of consistency and patience, your pup will learn exactly where to go.

Socialization and Training

SOCIALIZATION

Introducing your puppy to a variety of people, places, and things is essential in preventing behavioral problems, such as shyness or aggression, from developing later on.

"If the dog misses the opportunity throughout the first six months of his life to be extensively socialized on a daily basis, trying to make up for it later on can be very challenging—if not impossible," says Robin Kovary, director of the American Dog Trainers Network.

Socializing your puppy means introducing him to the world. Car rides, shopping malls, and noisy vacuums are all things that we're used to, but to your puppy, everything's new and a little bit scary.

When your puppy is nine weeks old, start by slowly introducing him to different people, one at a time. Gradually increase the number of adults and children he sees at once. It's important that your puppy sees men and women, as well as different ages and races. Puppies that grow up around just women, for example, may show fear and aggression when introduced later to men.

Another good way to socialize your puppy is with weekly trips to an outdoor shopping mall. He'll be able to see crowds of people, as well as strollers, wheelchairs, and bicycles.

Avoid dog parks, which can be high-risk areas for disease, until your puppy has had all his shots, usually around 16 weeks of age. After that, you'll find that these large grassy enclosures are a great place for him—and you—to make new friends.

Socialize your puppy at a young age to prevent behavioral problems later in life, such as shyness or fear.

Gentle handling on a daily basis will prepare your puppy for his first visit to the veterinarian or groomer.

Daily handling is also an essential part of the socialization process. Gently petting and touching different parts of his body, like his ears, paws, muzzle, and tail, will prepare him for his first trip to the veterinarian or groomer.

BASIC TRAINING

How Dogs Learn

Dogs learn by positive and negative reinforcement. Positive reinforcement encourages a dog to repeat a certain behavior by rewarding him after he does something you want. The reward can be food, toys, or praise. Negative reinforcement is an unpleasant consequent meant to discourage a particular behavior. This should never be in the form of physical abuse or cause any type of pain. Punishment is always humane, for example, a "time-out" where the dog is isolated for a short period of time from social contact.

Make training sessions fun and interesting for your puppy so that he looks forward to learning. Remember to praise your puppy for a job well done.

When using positive and negative reinforcement, consistency and timing are extremely important. For example, if you're teaching Fido to sit on command, use the same word every time. Once he follows your command, immediately give him a treat.

Consistency and timing can also work against you if you're not careful. For example, your dog may be afraid of thunder and after a big bang, you immediately pet him—that's positive reinforcement. You've essentially told your dog that it's okay to be afraid of thunder. Another example is catching Bowser digging a big hole in the backyard. You call him to you, then punish him. What's wrong with that? Bad timing. Dogs connect reward and punishment with the last thing they did. Now your dog thinks he's being punished for coming to you—not for digging.

First Thing First

Teaching your puppy his name is one of the easiest things to do, yet many owners don't do it right. They use a dog's name as a reprimand or as a precursor to punishment. A puppy's name should always be used in a positive manner. He should respond enthusiastically, without fear or hesitation.

To teach Fido to respond to his name, start off by saying it, then giving a food treat. Puppies can learn their names in about a week. After Fido starts responding consistently, the food treats should be phased out and replaced with petting or verbal praise.

OBEDIENCE

Within the first few weeks of bringing your puppy home, you can teach him basic obedience commands like come, sit, stay, and down. Training sessions should be kept short and sweet (one to three minutes per session, one to five times per day). Keep in mind that there's more than one way to train a puppy. If the methods below don't work, try a different approach or consult a professional trainer.

Come

Coming when called is one of the most important commands to teach your new puppy. Not only will it keep him out of dangerous situations (away from speeding cars, wild animals, or aggressive neighborhood pets), but there's nothing more frustrating then being ignored by your dog.

Teaching your dog to obey the come command could keep him away from dangerous situations, like speeding cars or aggressive neighborhood dogs.

Start by attaching a 15-foot cord to his collar. Then, with your dog standing several feet away, pull him gently toward you. As he comes closer, encourage him. Once he is by your side, praise him warmly. Repeat this several times.

Next, when you pull slightly on the cord and your dog starts coming to you, say "Come" at the same time. Always reward him for correct behavior with praise or a treat. Repeat this exercise until your dog comes to you on his own.

Sit

Put a treat in your hand and then place it in front of your dog's nose. Slowly raise your hand above his head while giving the command, "Sit." This will make his head reach up to sniff your hand while causing his hindquarters to rest on the ground. When he sits, praise him and immediately give him the treat. In the beginning, treats should be given consistently. Over time, however, the food reward should be phased out and replaced with warm praise.

Stay

The sit and stay commands go hand in hand. Have your puppy sit and then you should begin to back away slowly, encouraging him to stay. If he gets up and runs toward you, say "No" in a stern voice and bring him back to the original spot to start over. When the puppy remains sitting for a short period of time, give him a treat and lots of praise. Slowly increase the amount of time he needs to remain still in order to get the treat.

Down

Start by having your dog sit. Then, with a treat in your hand, make a downward motion in front of his nose as you say "Down." Only give him the treat if he obeys. Most puppies will need a little encouragement. If your pup won't go down on his own, hold the treat in front of his nose, tell him to go down, and apply light pressure to his shoulders while sweeping his front legs gently forward. Even if you had to assist him, praise him and give him the treat for obeying. Your puppy will soon learn that the command is not optional and will begin lying down on his own.

HOW TO SELECT A TRAINER

Anyone can claim to be a dog trainer. There are no federal or state requirements that have to be met. All someone needs is an ad from the yellow pages and they're in business. That's why it's important to do a little investigating when looking for a trainer. You need to put on your detective hat and find out about the following points before choosing one for your dog.

Reputation

Ask friends and co-workers who they use. Veterinary offices are also good sources, but ask if the doctor or staff know the trainer personally or if his business cards sitting on the counter were just dropped off.

Experience

Find out how long the trainer has been in business locally and where he received his training. If he's new to the area, find out what city and state he last worked. You can then call the local ASPCA, humane society, animal control agency, or a veterinarian in that area to find out about the trainer's reputation.

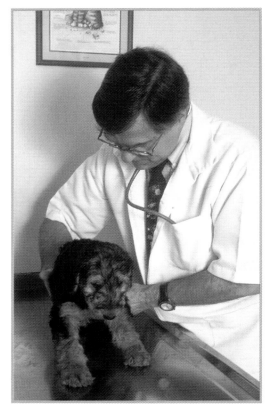

Friends, co-workers, and your veterinarian are good sources for finding reputable trainers.

Observe some training classes before you enroll your puppy to get a good idea of the trainer's style and his or her methods of teaching.

Training Method

Most trainers use key words or phrases, such as positive reinforcement or problem solving, but these can mean different things to different trainers. Find out exactly what is meant by these statements. Also, find out if the trainer just does leash training or will give you a working knowledge of behavior and manners.

Education

Find out if the trainer stays up-to-date on the latest techniques and information by attending workshops, conferences, and seminars.

Conduct

Visit the class before enrolling your dog. Observing the trainer in action will give you a good idea if he or she really loves working with dogs. Gentle but effective handling methods should always be used, and both animals and owners should be treated with respect. Most importantly, trust your instincts. If you see the trainer do anything you're not comfortable with, find someone else.

References

Don't just ask for the list—call! Find out what each person on the list did or did not like about the trainer or class.

Affiliation

Find out if the trainer is a member of a professional organization. These associations are joined voluntarily and work on educating members on the latest industry standards. The National Association of Dog Obedience Instructors, for example, reviews a trainer's qualifications to make sure they provide competent instruction and use humane methods of training. For a referral in your area, contact one of the following professional organizations: American Dog Trainers Network at 212-727-7257, or visit the website at http://www.inch.com/~dogs/index.htm; Association of Pet Dog Trainers at 800-PET-DOGS, or visit the website at http://www.apdt.com.

BEHAVIORISTS

If your pet is having problems such as aggression, destructiveness, housesoiling, marking, spraying, self-mutilation, or excessive vocalization, you'll want to seek help from a certified animal behaviorist.

"At least half of what a behaviorist does is educate the client about the behavior," explained Dr. Nicholas Dodman, a board-certified veterinary behaviorist and director of Tufts Behavior Clinic. "They teach the owner why the dog or cat is behaving that way so they can understand and deal with the problem."

By looking at an animal's lifestyle (exercise, diet, appropriate outlets for natural behaviors), a behaviorist can develop a treatment program, which may include medication. What kind of treatment program and how long until results are seen varies according to the nature and severity of the problem.

There are two ways a behaviorist can become titled. A veterinarian can become board certified by the American College of Veterinary Behavior, which includes testing and a residency. The other way is through the Animal Behavior Society of the United States. This certification is for people who are not veterinarians but usually have doctorates.

Currently there are only 125 certified behaviorists in the United States. Many of the larger veterinary schools, like Tufts University, have on-staff behaviorists that offer expert advice directly to owners or their veterinarian. Before seeking help, however, your pet should be given a complete physical exam to make sure that there are no underlying health problems. Something as simple as arthritis, for example, can make a pet irritable and aggressive.

A behaviorist can help curb negative behavior patterns in a dog, such as aggression, destructiveness, or excessive barking. This baby Lab is on his best behavior for the camera.

Tufts Behavior Clinic also offers the Petfax program, in which owners throughout the country can get advice on how to correct problems in their cats and other pets. After filling out a questionnaire, owners receive a written report that includes a diagnosis and a personalized treatment plan for correcting the problem. The client also has the opportunity to speak directly with the behaviorist several times during the two months following the Petfax consultation.

Consultation forms can be obtained by phone (508-839-8PET); by mail (Behavior Clinic, Tufts School of Veterinary Medicine, 200 Westboro Road, North Grafton, MA 01536); or online (www.tufts.edu/vet/petfax). There is a basic consultation fee.

Another option is the Animal Behavior Clinic at Cornell University in Ithaca, New York. Appointments must be made in advance. For dogs, a telephone consultation takes about two hours. Problems will be diagnosed and the owner instructed on methods to reduce frequency and severity of the problem. If necessary, drugs will be prescribed. A letter outlining the treatment will be sent to the referring veterinarian. To make an appointment, call Dr. Vint Virga (607) 253-3844 or Dr. Katherine Houpt (607) 253-3450.

Also, the San Francisco SPCA's Behavior Help Line (415-554-3075) is free and offers pet owners step-by-step instruction on how to modify behaviors such as barking, digging, house soiling, and biting.

FUN, FUN, FUN

Frisbee, flyball, and agility clubs around the country are a great way for you and your puppy to have fun. You may have caught a glimpse of one of these increasingly popular canine sports on television. The following is a brief description of each and how to get involved.

Agility is a sport that allows mixed breeds and purebred dogs of all ages to compete. This Vizsla soars through the tire jump with ease.

Agility

Agility is a sport in which the handler directs a dog over a timed obstacle course. Mixed and purebred dogs of all ages are allowed to compete. They race against the clock as they jump hurdles, scale ramps, burst through tunnels, traverse a seesaw, and weave through a line of poles. Scoring is based on faults similar to equestrian show jumping. The United States Dog Agility Association (USDAA) has established four basic competitive classes based on jump heights. Dogs measuring over 16 inches in height must jump in the 24-inch or 30-inch class. For dogs 16 inches or less in height, there are two classes of

Puppies are a great source of fun and are usually willing to do most anything, provided that you are there with them.

Most dogs enjoy agility because the obstacles are easy to learn, and it doesn't require a tremendous amount of training like other competitive canine activities.

competition—the 12-inch and 18-inch class. Dogs measuring over 12 inches high but not more than 16 inches must jump in the 18-inch class. The different height classes were developed to provide safe but challenging jumps that are fair in competitions.

The best way to see if your dog will enjoy agility is to try it. Most dogs do well because the obstacles are relatively easy to learn, and it doesn't require hours of training like some other competitive canine activities. To learn more about agility competitions or clubs in your area, contact The United States Dog Agility Association at (972) 231-9700 or visit the website at http://www.usdaa.com.

Flyball

Flyball was started in California in the late 1970s by Herbert Wagner, who first demonstrated it on the Johnny Carson Show. Today the sport is widely played throughout the country. Flyball is a relay race with four dogs on a team. The game is played on a 51-foot course that consists of 4 hurdles spaced 10 feet apart and a spring-loaded box that shoots out a tennis ball. Each dog jumps the hurdles, steps on the box, and catches the tennis ball, then races back over the hurdles to the starting line. Then it starts all over again with the next dog. The first team to have all four dogs run without errors wins the heat. To find out about clubs in your area or tournament information, contact the North American Flyball Association at 1400 W. Devon Ave., #512, Chicago, Ill. 60660 or visit the website at http://muskie.fishnet.com/~flyball/flyball.html.

Frisbee

It all started back in the mid-70s when Alex Stein crashed a Dodgers baseball game with his Frisbee dog "Ashley Whippet" and performed a high-flying demonstration in front of a nationwide audience. The crowd loved it, and the sport of canine Frisbee was born.

Competitions held throughout the country, like the Alpo Canine Frisbee Disc Championships, are divided into beginner and intermediate levels, each consisting of two different events. The first is called the Mini-Distance. It's played on a 20-yard field and competitors are given 60 seconds to make as many throws and catches as possible.

The second is the freeflight event, which consists of a choreographed series of acrobatic moves to music. Judges award points on a one to ten scale in each of the following categories: degree of difficulty, execution, leaping agility, and showmanship. Bonus points can be given to competitors with spectacular or innovative freeflight moves.

Mixed or purebred dogs can compete. A good canine Frisbee competitor should have strong retrieval and tracking instincts, an even temperament, a lean build, and sound hips.

Friskies/ALPO sponsors over 100 community contests throughout the country each year. To find out more about competitions in your area or for a free Frisbee training manual call 888-444-ALPO or visit the website at www.friskies.com.

Junior Showmanship

A great way for children to get involved in showing dogs is through the Junior Showmanship program. Children ages 10 through 18 can compete and are judged on their ability to present or handle their dogs. The quality of their presentation, not the dog, is judged. Juniors are encouraged to develop their handling abilities, dress appropriately, conduct themselves in a proper manner, and present their dog in a well-groomed condition. The dogs must be owned by the child or a member of the child's family.

Some local dog clubs offer weekly handling classes. These informal sessions afford both dog and handler an opportunity to practice in a setting similar to an actual show. For more information contact the American Kennel Club at 919-854-0195 or visit the website at www.akc.org.

If you want to enter your dog in Frisbee competitions, he must have strong retrieval and tracking instincts, an even temperament, a lean build, and sound hips.

Health Care

SELECTING A VETERINARIAN

When choosing a veterinarian for your puppy, you'll need to do a little detective work to find the right professional who is knowledgeable, friendly, and caring.

Start off by asking friends, co-workers, and neighbors who they use. This usually ends up being your best source but don't just accept the answer, "I use this doctor." Find out exactly what they like and dislike about the veterinarian. A state or local veterinary association will also give referrals of professionals in your area.

Once you have several names, find out if they are in good standing with the American Animal Hospital Association, which requires its members to maintain high medical care standards. Each hospital that belongs to the AAHA completes a detailed evaluation of its services and equipment. A trained consultant then inspects the hospital in the areas of emergency services, surgery and anesthesia, radiology services, pathology services, nursing care, pharmacy, dentistry, examination facilities, medical library, and housekeeping. Less than 18 percent of small veterinary hospitals in the United States and Canada are accredited. To contact the American Animal Hospital Association call 800-252-2242 or visit their website at http://www.healthypet.com.

Now that you have a few solid leads to go on, visit each clinic or hospital before making an appointment. Look for an office that is well lit and smells clean. Introduce yourself to the receptionist and explain that you're looking for a new veterinarian. You'll need to ask a lot of questions while you're there, such as: How long has the veterinarian been in practice? Does he or she specialize in a certain species? Does the doctor participate in seminars and conferences on the latest developments in veterinary medicine? Does the hospital provide 24-hour care? Are they open nights and weekends for appointments? Do they offer a convenient payment policy? After visiting several places you'll have a good idea of which doctor you'd like to use.

First Visit

For the first appointment, bring a detailed record of your pet's medical history including date of birth, medications currently being taken, and vaccinations received. This information will prevent repeating tests or treatments.

After the examination, evaluate the veterinarian. Were you and your pet greeted warmly? Was a thorough nose-to-tail exam given? Could you communicate easily with the veterinarian? Were all your questions answered courteously? If any treatment or medication was given, did the doctor explain why? If you answered "No" to any of these questions, look for another veterinarian.

PREVENTATIVE CARE

A veterinary checkup once a year can help catch health problems before they become serious. However, your puppy should be brought in if you see any of the following signs: coughing, vomiting, severe scratching or biting, decreased appetite, limping, difficulty getting up or lying down, abnormal discharge from nose or eyes, or any unusual behavior, such as being sluggish or suddenly vicious.

Vaccinations

Vaccinations are an important part of keeping your puppy healthy because they protect him against a variety of illnesses. At two, three, and four months of age, puppies should be given a 5-in-1 vaccine, which provides protection from distemper, parvovirus, hepatitis, parainfluenza, and leptospirosis. Rottweilers, Doberman Pinschers, and Pit Bulls need to be vaccinated again at five months of age. When this series of

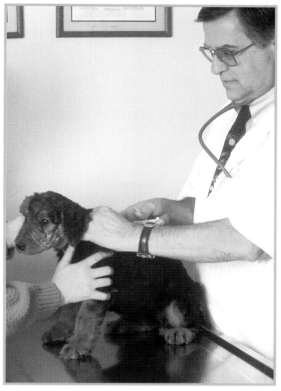

It's important that you take your dog's vaccination schedule with you on your first visit to the vet.

vaccinations is complete, an annual booster is given. The type of booster given depends on where you live. In general, dogs should be vaccinated for distemper, hepatitis, leptospirosis, parvovirus, bordetella (kennel cough), and rabies. Your veterinarian may also recommend other vaccines to protect against Lymedisease and coronavirus.

Rabies

Throughout most of the country, rabies vaccinations are required by law. Puppies are vaccinated at 12 and 64 weeks of age. Annual boosters are then required in high-risk regions, like the mid-Atlantic, while in other parts of the country, it's only needed every three years.

Rabies is a deadly virus that attacks the brain. It's passed in the saliva from an infected animal when it bites another animal or person. Rabid pets show an unexplained change in behavior. For example, a dog that's normally friendly will turn aggressive. Other signs include loss of appetite, weakness, seizures, or sudden death. Because raccoons, bats, skunks, and foxes are common carriers, it's important to keep your dog on a leash while he is outside to avoid an encounter.

A healthy dog that bites a person will usually be confined for ten days by Animal Control and observed by a veterinarian for signs of the illnesses.

If signs that are suggestive of rabies develop, the animal will be euthanized and brain tissue samples will be taken for examination.

Lyme Disease

Lyme disease is a bacterial infection transmitted by ticks that can damage joints, kidneys, and other tissues. The highest incidences occur in the Northeast, from Massachusetts to Maryland; North Central states, especially Wisconsin and Minnesota; and on the West Coast, particularly northern California.

If you live in a high-risk area, your puppy should be vaccinated at 12 and 15 weeks of age, then yearly. Not all animals exposed to Lyme disease develop clinical symptoms. Generally, those that do have soreness and lameness of joints, fever, and loss of appetite.

Keeping your dog on a leash when he is outside will keep him safe and prevent him from coming into contact with other animals.

How to Prevent Lyme Disease

—Have your puppy vaccinated.

—Use veterinarian prescribed tick collars, spray, and dips.

—Avoid areas where deer ticks are abundant (wooded areas and fields in endemic regions).

—Check your puppy daily for ticks and remove any promptly. Ticks are best removed with tweezers. Grasp as close to the skin as possible then gently pull backward.

—Save suspicious ticks in a jar or bag with a blade of grass for identification.

Parvovirus

Canine parvovirus is a highly contagious and often deadly virus that causes intestinal hemorrhaging. Clinical signs include lethargy, loss of appetite, severe vomiting, and bloody diarrhea. While parvo can affect all dogs, Rottweilers, Doberman Pinschers, and Pit Bulls are more susceptible.

To prevent your puppy from getting parvo, he should be kept away from public places and from dogs whose vaccine histories are unknown until all of his vaccinations have been given. This is usually around five months of age.

SPAYING AND NEUTERING

Spaying is a surgical procedure that removes a female's ovaries and uterus. Neutering removes a male's testicles. Both birth control operations are safe and require minimal hospitalization. Because dogs can start reproducing around six months of age, many veterinarians recommend sterilization at four months of age to prevent an accidental litter. Besides helping control the pet overpopulation, spaying and neutering is good for a dog's health.

Neutering prevents testicular cancer, prostate disease, and hernias, as well as reduces aggression in males. Spaying helps prevent pyometra (a pus-filled uterus) and breast cancer, which is fatal in 50 percent of female dogs. To reduce the odds of your puppy getting breast cancer, she should be spayed before her first heat, which is about six months of age. Besides the health benefits, fixed pets live two to three times longer on average than those not fixed.

The cost of surgery depends on the sex and weight of a dog. Check with your local humane society or city shelter to see if they offer a low-cost service. If you can't afford to spay or neuter your pet, some local humane groups offer financial assistance.

Listed below are myths and misconceptions owners have about spaying and neutering.

Myth: An altered dog will not protect the house.

Fact: Not a chance! Your dog will still have every desire to defend his home.

Myth: Only females need to be fixed.

Fact: The old saying, "It takes two to tango" is as true for animals as it is for humans. A male pet can easily father 750 offspring in his lifetime.

Myth: My pet will become fat and lazy if he's neutered.

Fact: Overfeeding and lack of exercise make companion animals fat and lazy—not the surgery.

Myth: Children should witness the miracle of birth.

Fact: Teach your children about reproduction in a more responsible manner. There are plenty of good books and videos available.

Myth: A female should be spayed after her first litter.

Fact: No, don't wait. By doing it sooner, rather than later, she'll be healthier and live longer.

FLEAS

They're pesky and persistent. Even if your animal never steps one paw outside, he can still become infested with these tiny, black, bloodsucking insects. Fleas can enter your home through cracks, crevasses, screen doors—even by hitching a ride on your clothes.

Throughout most of the country, fleas flourish during the summer when temperatures are around 65 to 80 degrees and the humidity is high. But in some areas, like Florida, it's just the opposite. Flea season occurs during the winter months. There are exceptions, however. High-altitude regions, like Denver, or the dry deserts of Southern California and Arizona, are flea free. Unfortunately, by the time you see the first flea, you're already outnumbered. Adult fleas on your pet account for just five percent of the total population hiding in the house. This means that you'll need a serious plan of attack—fast. Start by vacuuming the areas where your dog spends the most time, like his bed or favorite chair. You'll need to do this at least once a week. Bedding should also be washed in hot, soapy water and dried on the high-heat setting. Don't stop there; you'll need to thoroughly clean the entire house—inside and out. Sweep all floors, patios, and steps. Vacuum rugs and furniture, paying special attention to cracks and crevices where fleas could be hiding. Change the vacuum bag frequently, because fleas love to breed in dark, warm places. (Placing part of a flea collar inside the vacuum bag

Ticks can transmit illnesses such as Rocky Mountain Spotted Fever, ehrlichiosis, and Lyme disease. Keep your puppy out of grassy or wooded areas during the spring and summer months.

A heartworm preventative, provided by your veterinarian, can help prevent your dog from contracting this dangerous parasite.

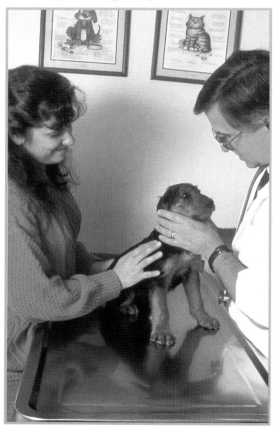

will kill the adult fleas that get sucked up.) Once your house is clean, the next step is to find an effective flea-control product. This has been made easy over recent years by the introduction of several "spot-on" formulas. These liquid products come in premeasured vials and are applied directly onto your puppy's skin. The product keeps pets free of fleas for one month. Because there are several spot-on formulas on the market, find out what brand your veterinarian recommends.

TICKS

These small parasites can cause big problems for pets by transmitting illnesses such as Rocky Mountain Spotted Fever, ehrlichiosis, and Lyme disease. Luckily, the same spot-on treatment used to protect against fleas works on ticks, too.

Ticks are usually found in grassy or wooded areas during the spring and summer months. Even if you're using a product that protects against ticks, it's still wise to check your dog around the head, neck, ears, and feet after he's been outside. If you find a tick, remove it immediately. Don't use petroleum jelly or try burning it off with a match, which can hurt your pet. Instead, grasp the tick as close to the skin as possible with fine-point tweezers and gently pull straight out. Apply antiseptic on the bite area to prevent inflammation. Dispose of the tick by flushing it down the toilet or drowning it in alcohol.

HEARTWORM

If you live in an area that has mosquitos, your pet can get heartworm.

Your pet can become infested with pesky fleas even if he never goes outside. Be sure the areas where your dog spends the most time are clean and flea-free.

Heartworm is transmitted through mosquito bites. From this, a parasite (dirofilaria immitis) settles in the heart and can grow to 14 inches in length. If not removed, it can cause permanent heart and lung damage, even death.

Incidents of heartworm have been found in all 50 states. According to the American Heartworm Society, the highest infection rate in dogs—up to 45 percent of those not on preventative medication—occurs within 150 miles of the Atlantic and Gulf coasts and along the Mississippi River.

Dogs housed outside are up to five times more likely to be infected than those that stay indoors. Even so, inside dogs still need to take preventative medication.

Clinical signs of heartworm infestation include coughing, exercise intolerance, abnormal lung sounds, difficulty breathing, enlargement of the liver, fainting episodes, fluid accumulation in the abdominal cavity, and an abnormal heartbeat.

Most dogs in the early stages have no outward signs of disease, which is why your veterinarian will need to run a blood test to determine if heartworm is present. Medication is available for preventing heartworm as well as treating it.

DENTAL CARE

Regular dental care is vital to your pet's overall health, yet it is often the most neglected. According to the American Veterinary Dental Society, 80 percent of dogs show signs of oral disease by the time they're three years old. Warning signs include bad breath, yellow-brown tartar buildup around the gums, difficulty chewing, and pawing at the face or mouth.

If plaque and tartar buildup is not removed on a regular basis, it could lead to periodontal disease, which, when left untreated, causes tooth loss. Periodontal disease may also cause bacteria and toxins to enter the bloodstream infecting organs such as the heart, liver, and kidneys.

Certain breeds, such as Poodles, Terriers, Greyhounds, and Collies, are more prone to periodontal disease because they have less tooth-supporting bone. Flat-faced breeds, like Bulldogs, also have a problem, because their crowded mouths make it easier for plaque to build up on teeth.

Your dog's oral care is just as important as his grooming or nutritional needs. Have his teeth checked at least once a year by your veterinarian.

The best way to prevent dental disease is to brush your pet's teeth daily. While this might be idealistic, it's not very realistic. Shoot for once a week using a soft bristled toothbrush, cotton swab, or gauze pad with toothpaste specially formulated for animals. Avoid using human toothpaste, which can cause an upset stomach.

A tooth-friendly diet is also important. Look for dog food brands with the "Seal of Acceptance from the Veterinary Oral Health Council." These specially formulated foods have been proven to reduce accumulation of plaque and tartar.

PET INSURANCE

Statistics show that two out of three pets will experience major medical problems. The high cost of some veterinary procedures, which can run into thousands of dollars, has forced owners that don't have the financial means to make tough decisions: Watch their pet suffer or end his life through euthanasia. It doesn't have to be that way. To help

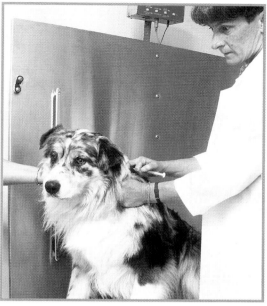

Unfortunately, veterinary bills can become quite expensive. Today, many pet owners are investing in pet insurance to ensure that their dog can be well taken care of.

defray expenses, more and more owners are turning to insurance for their pets. There are several companies throughout the United States that offer this type of insurance. Veterinary Pet Insurance (VPI) is the largest, with more than 850,000 clients. It operates just like a traditional human health care insurance plan. Owners can go to any licensed veterinarian, veterinary specialist, or animal hospital in the world. To find out more about pet insurance, ask your veterinarian, call VPI at 800-872-7387, or visit the website at www.veterinarypetinsurance.com.

POISON CONTROL

The chemicals we use to clean our houses, get rid of bugs, and keep our yards green can make our pets sick.

"Somehow people have the idea that their pets won't get into anything that's harmful to them, and that's just not right," says Dr. Jay Albertson from the ASPCA's National Animal Poison Control Center in Illinois. "They'll get into just about everything."

Approximately 85 percent of all calls to the Poison Control Center involve accidental exposure within the home. "A little common sense goes a long way," says Albertson. He recommends keeping household cleaners or other dangerous products up high and out of reach. Ant or roach baits should be put in an area inaccessible to your pet. When treating the house for fleas or ticks, read the label carefully and follow instructions. There have even been cases, says Albertson, where owners have inadvertently given their pet medication meant for themselves. To avoid confusion, keep your pet's medication in a separate cabinet.

Some less likely poisoning culprits (but just as dangerous) are houseplants.

Nibbling on the wrong plant can cause severe mouth and throat irritation or an upset stomach. Avoid planting oleanders, azaleas, rhododendrons, and Japanese yew in the yard. If eaten, these plants can cause an upset stomach or diarrhea.

Keep pets off grassy areas that have just been treated with fertilizer or weed killers. If your pet is exposed, wash his feet with mild soap and warm water. If you live in an apartment or condominium complex that provides outside maintenance, find out when the gardening service treats areas with chemicals. In garages, keep car-cleaning products, antifreeze, and windshield washer fluids stored high on shelves.

If you suspect that your pet has been exposed to a poison, contact your veterinarian immediately. Signs include difficulty breathing or unconsciousness. If your pet is not in immediate danger, contact the Poison Control Center, which gives advice 24 hours a day, 7 days a week. Specific recommendations are given by one of ten veterinary toxicologists on staff. When you call, be prepared to give the following information about the exposure (amount, type, time occurred), the species (breed, age, sex, weight), and the problem it's experiencing.

The Center can be reached at 800-548-2423 or 888-426-4435. There is a fee per case that can be charged on your credit card. If you do not have a credit card, call 900-680-0000. The charge will appear on your telephone bill.

IDENTIFICATION

Keeping identification tags on your puppy is his ticket home if he becomes lost. Besides using tags, which can easily fall off, consider microchipping your puppy. It provides a permanent and positive form of identification that cannot be lost, altered, or intentionally removed.

A tiny computer chip the size of a rice grain is programmed with a unique identification number and injected under the skin of your pet (between the shoulder blades of dogs). The procedure is no more painful than a vaccination and can be done at your veterinarian's office while you wait.

Keep identification tags on your dog's collar in case he should become separated from you.

Most city and private shelters have hand-held scanners and check every animal that comes through their doors. The scanner reveals the chip's maker and encoded identification number. With this information, shelter workers can call a manufacturer's 24-hour registry to get the owner's name and phone number. For more information, talk to your veterinarian.

HEALTH CARE

Here's a guide to some common plants and foods that are toxic to animals.

C ......**cardiovascular toxin**
GI ....**gastrointestinal toxin**
R ......**respiratory toxin**
N ......**neurological toxin**
KO ..**kidney/organ failure**
***........dangerous and can be fatal**

Alcohol . . . . .N
Almonds* (kernel in the
    pit contain cyanide) . . . . .R
Amaryllis bulb* . . . . .GI, N
Anthurium* . . . . .KO
Apricot* (kernel in the pit
    contains cyanide) . . . . .R
Autumn crocus* (Colchicum
    autumnale) very poisonous . . . . . .GI, C
Avocado* (leaves, seeds, stem,
    skin) fatal to birds . . . . .C, KO
Azalea (entire rhododendron
    family) . . . . .C, GI, N
Begonia* . . . . .KO
Bird of Paradise . . . . .GI
Bittersweet . . . . .GI
Bleeding heart* C
Boxwood . . . . .GI
Bracken fern .N
Buckeye . . . . .GI, N
Buttercup (Ranunculus) . . . . .GI
Caffeine . . . . .GI, N
Caladium* . . . . .KO
Calla lily . . . . .KO
Castor bean* (can be fatal
    if chewed) . . . . .GI, C, N
Cherry (kernel in the pit
    contains cyanide) . . . . .R
Chinese sacred or heavenly
    bamboo* contains cyanide . . . . .R
Chocolate* . . . . .GI, N
Choke cherry, unripe berries*
    contains cyanide . . . . .R
Chrysanthemum
    (a natural source of pyrethrins) . .GI, N
Clemati . . . . .GI
Crocus bulb . . . . .GI, N
Croton (Codiaeum sp.) . . . . .GI
Cyclamen bulb . . . . .GI
Delphinium, larkspur, monkshood* . . . .N
Dumb cane (Dieffenbachia)*
    contains cyanide . . . . .GI, R

Elderberry, unripe berries*
    contains cyanide . . . . .R
English ivy (All Hedera
    species of ivy) . . . . .GI
Fig (Ficus) General allergan, dermatitis
Four-o'clocks (Mirabilis) . . . . .GI
Foxglove (Digitalis)* can be fatal C
Garlic* (raw or spoiled) . . . . .GI
Hyacinth bulbs . . . . .GI
Hydrangea* contains cyanide . . . . .R
Holly berries .GI
Iris corms . . . . .GI
Jack-in-the-pulpit* . . . . .KO
Jimson weed* . . . . .R
Kalanchoe* can be fatal C
Lantana* (liver failure) . . . . .KO
Lily (bulbs of most species) . . . . .GI
Lily-of-the-valley can be fatal* C
Lupine species . . . . .N
Marijuana or hemp
    (Cannabis)* can be fatal . . . . .N, GI
Milkweed* C
Mistletoe berries* shock . . . . .N, C
Morning glory* Seeds toxic
    to birds . . . . .N
Mountain laurel C
Narcissus, daffodil (Narcissus) . . . . . . .GI
Oak* (remove bark for use
    as a bird perch) . . . . .KO
Oleander* very poisonous,
    can be fatal C
Onions* (raw or spoiled) . . . . .GI
Peach* (kernel in the pit
    contains cyanide) . . . . .R
Pencil cactus/plant* (Euphorbia
    sp.) dermatitis . . . . .GI
Philodendron (all species)* . . . . .KO
Poinsettia (many hybrids,
    avoid them all), dermatitis . . . . .GI
Potato (leaves and stem) . . . . .GI, N
Rhubarb leaves* . . . . .KO
Rosary Pea (Arbus sp.)* . . . . .GI, C, N
Scheffelera (umbrella plant) . . . . .KO
Shamrock (Oxalis sp.) . . . . .KO
Spurge (Euphorbia sp.) . . . . .GI
Tomatoes (leaves and stem) . . . . . . .GI, N
Yew*, fatal to most animals C

Reprinted with permission of the American Animal
Hospital Association.

Suggested Reading

Hart, Ernest H., *The Guide to Owning a Puppy.* RE 304
Neptune City, NJ: T.F.H. Publications, Inc.
Concisely written for the new puppy owner, this informative, detailed, easy-to-follow book will lead the reader through the important first steps of raising a puppy into a happy and healthy canine companion. A must-have for all first-time puppy owners.

Koler-Matznick, Janice, *The Guide to Handraising Puppies.* RE 347
Neptune City, NJ: T.F.H. Publications, Inc.
Animal behaviorist and dog trainer Janice Koler-Matznick brings her years of experience to this complete guide on raising orphaned litters and single puppies by hand. This easy-to-read book concentrates on assisting the reader with raising physically and psychologically healthy puppies.

Kennedy, Katharine, *Housebreaking and Other Puppy Problems.* RD 073
Neptune City, NJ: T.F.H. Publications, Inc.
This book helps the new puppy owner prepare for and deal with every potential problem, from housebreaking to excessive chewing. Most importantly, it discusses how to solve these problems when all else fails. The relationship between the puppy and his new family can be less stressful and lots more fun using the helpful tips in this book.

DePrisco, Andrew, *A New Owner's Guide to Training the Perfect Puppy.* JG 109
Neptune City, NJ: T.F.H. Publications, Inc.
Author Andrew DePrisco takes you by the collar and leads you through everything you need to know about parenting a puppy. This book makes it possible to communicate with your new puppy, initiate the first lessons with success, select the best supplies, and choose the correct training approach for your purebred or mixed-breed puppy.

Mahood, Jan, *Adopting a Dog.* WW 069
Neptune City, NJ: T.F.H. Publications, Inc.
Adopting a Dog provides the support and resources you'll need to find the right dog for you and your family, covering everything from how to choose the type of dog that best fits your lifestyle, to visiting a shelter, contacting rescue agencies, and searching the Internet. This book will help start you on the road to successful dog ownership, as well as teach you how to care for and train your newly adopted pet.

Fields, Mia, *Puppy Care and Training.* RD 086
Neptune City, NJ: T.F.H. Publications, Inc.
Raising a puppy into a healthy and happy adult dog is a big responsibility. It's important that a new puppy owner knows the basic steps and tools needed to care for a small puppy. This book expertly guides the new owner through all the stages of a puppy's growth and explains how to deal with common behavior problems through training. All puppy owners should have this book on their shelves.